Lens and Life

A Visual Autobiography

By

Viktória Farkas

Lens & Life

Table of Contents

Chapter 1

An Expedition Through Shifting Sands - From Siófok to Self-
Discovery   1

Chapter 2

Focus and Frame- Capturing Dreams in Pixels   8

Chapter 3

Exploring more-Finding Freedom Beyond Comfort   17

Chapter 4

Love in the City That Never Sleeps - A New Beginning   23

Chapter 5

Dreams Unlimited in NYC- Through the Lens of Love   30

Chapter 6

A Photographic Journey of Self-Discovery - Ups and Downs   41

Chapter 7

A World of Art and Photography - Beauty, Gratitude and
Adventure   50

Chapter 8

The Wow Factor - Elevating Photography Beyond
Expectations   60

Chapter 9

The Art of Editing - A Thing of Beauty is a Joy Forever   72

Chapter 10

Sky's the limit - Following all your dreams   77

Chapter 1

An Expedition Through Shifting Sands - From Siófok to Self-Discovery

The auditorium was packed with energy, a vibrant band of sound and movement. Every corner was adorned with eager faces, a sea of anticipation rippling through the air. The applause began as I took the stage, and a symphony of encouragement and admiration filled me with boundless joy.

With each step, I gave up on the music, and my body was twirling in joy and devotion. At that moment, nothing else existed but the dance – every leap and every twirl. The only thing I could hear was music and loud cheers from the crowd.

But no, there was something else, too. A sweet yet insistent voice pierced through, calling my name tenderly. "Viktória, Vick! Wake up, honey!" Reality began to intrude upon my fantasy. The distant echoes of applause started fading into the background, and a single voice emerged, pulling me back to the waking world.

Opening my eyes, I found myself greeted by my mother's familiar face. She was smiling gently in the morning light. Though my dream had been interrupted, the memory lingered—a loving fragment of my early years was my enduring passion for dance.

Dancing in the light

From as far back as I can remember, I've been drawn to the world of art as naturally as if it were written in my DNA, and this is what you call a "BORN ARTIST." Perhaps it was my mother's skillful hand that first ignited this flame within me, her talent for drawing serving as an early inspiration that I couldn't help but inherit.

Unfortunately, I never dealt with it more deeply. I stayed with children's drawings, but I kept all my drawings. One of my favorite styles is mandala drawing. In the ancient Sanskrit language of Hinduism and Buddhism, mandala means "circle." Once, I read somewhere that, "Mandala is all about finding peace in the symmetry of the design and of the universe." I relate to it from an artist's perspective. My inner artist yearned for expression through various art forms, including dance. Yes, it was another passion of mine. You would hardly believe it, but my Mom often tells a story about me, telling me that I learned to dance before I learned to walk. I was so small that a dress had to be sewn for the performance. When I was little, I danced in a traditional German dance group. This was my first dance group in Bátaszék. My biggest fan and mentor was my dance teacher, János Glöckner. My sister also danced in this group.

Balaton lover

Before I begin my life story, let me introduce myself. I am Viktória Farkas, and my journey started in the picturesque town of Siófok, Hungary, nestled near the tranquil shores of Lake Balaton. I was born in 1987. Though we were not wealthy, my family had everything by the grace of the Lord. However, when I was just nine years old, the fabric of our family began to fray as my parents parted ways. After their divorce, we moved a lot. I lived with my mom and my older sister. I also have two younger brothers on my father's side. I didn't have too many friends. Maybe I couldn't make more friends due to too many traversed towns and schools. I attended eight grades of elementary school in 4 cities in 5 schools.

Relax in the nature

"The guitar is an orchestra in itself." - Ludwig van Beethoven

After my parents divorced, we moved to a small village, Vaskút. My mother's family lived there. It was so small. Everyone knew everyone. As I just said, I couldn't make many friends anywhere, but one interesting fact is I preferred to be friends with boys; I didn't get along very well with girls. My mom often said I was such a bad kid that ten boys would envy me. Throughout my life, I naturally gravitated towards male companionship, finding comfort and understanding in their company, where I struggled to connect with girls. I think having male friends is less drama, less dealing with emotional issues, and simply not complicated.

"Flowers don't tell; they show." - Stephanie Seem

But, as a matter of sad fact, I couldn't connect myself to my father. My relationship with him remained fraught with pain and distance. My father's parents lived so far from us; though we couldn't visit them as often as we wished, the summers spent in their company were like precious jewels in my memories' treasure. I remember the summers together with our cousins. Whenever we went in the summer, they took us to Lenti Beach.

My maternal grandparents were artisans of a different kind— they were bakers. Their bakery had a huge wood-burning furnace. I recall with fondness the countless hours spent exploring every nook and cranny of the bustling workroom, inhaling the intoxicating aroma of freshly baked bread that filled the air. I remember my grandfather teaching me how to draw a footprint in flour.

Anyway, back in my village, Vaskút, I ultimately found some friends there. As I told you earlier, I had a passion for dance. I was a member of a dance group with whom we often prepared small poetry, music, and dance performances. We performed in the village community center. We organized a Mother's Day show, a charity evening, or just showed that "we know this." We seized every chance to shine on stage.

"Forget your troubles and dance." - *Bob Marley*
The village community center became our sanctuary, the stage our canvas, as we poured our passion and creativity into each performance.

I also met my current life partner in this group. His presence added an extra sparkle to our shared adventures. Together, we danced through the chapters of our lives, finding support and joy in each other's company as we navigated the twists and turns of youth and beyond. From the innocent days of the village to the trials and triumphs of adulthood, we've witnessed each other's growth and evolution. We are life partners for a reason.

All my life there, I felt this village was small for me. I longed for something more. I wanted to explore the world.

After I finished elementary school, we moved to a smaller town. I went to economics school. I didn't want to go there, but my mom forced me to, and years later, I was very grateful. It was a sane decision indeed.

"A book is a gift you can open again and again." - Garrison Keillor

Majestic Lion King

Chapter 2

Focus and Frame- Capturing Dreams in Pixels

When you are a child, you often dream of the day you will finally grow up and escape the confines of childhood. You fantasize about a world free from the shackles of submitting strict routines and the monotony of school life. Little did you know, the true beauty of these carefree days would only become apparent growing up. I've always longed to break free from my small town's limitations and explore the world's wonders. Basically, I had an artistic mind who always wanted to wander in search of beauty, nature, and creativity.

American Goldfinch

Now, as I reflect on my journey, I realize that the essence of life lies not in grand adventures or exotic destinations but in the simple joys of embracing the present moment and finding beauty in the everyday. After graduating high school, I got a job as an office assistant in the city. I have been working since I was 18 years old. I was lucky because it was difficult in my small town to get an office job without experience. I got one, and I wanted to be good. I was young and enthusiastic.

9-11 Memorial light

That's when I realized my childhood love for art and drawing had turned into a passion for photography. Thus, I started choosing my phones based on their camera quality. I couldn't afford a professional camera, but, you know, photography has no rules. It is not a sport, So I started capturing images with my phone's camera.

Tatabánya Turul Monument

In the sky, there are no limits

When I used to take photos with my smartphone, I was content with the results. I never bothered with editing programs; I just relied on the built-in application. But now, I can clearly see the difference. After editing some old phone pictures with Photoshop, they look significantly better.

Epic sunset at Lake Balaton

Vessel Hudson Yard New York

Back when I started taking photos with a phone, one of my favorites was the Huawei. At the time, it had the best camera quality. Today, I am using an iPhone14, which I adore because of its primary 48MP camera and RAW option. With these features, I can edit my phone pictures to resemble those taken with a professional camera. So, even if I don't have my Sony camera with me, I still have a quality phone camera at my disposal. Of course, nothing beats the quality of a professional camera.

Türr lookout point, it's my favorite place to calm down

According to the famous Spanish painter Pablo Picasso, "Art is the elimination of the unnecessary."

The same principle applies to editing a picture. Like Picasso, I believe true art is correcting errors without altering its inherent beauty. The other name of this art is "creativity." Einstein said that,

"Creativity is seeing what others see and thinking what no one else ever thought."

This is precisely what I love to do. Enough about me; let me stop babbling and show you some of my work(edited with Photoshop) that I hold dear because they say, "A picture is worth a thousand words."

Chicago The Rookery's famous staircase

Heart shape from my favorite book

My favorite perfume, thanks to my friend

After my beloved photographic work, I would like to share some of my job experiences. As I told you, I got my first job as an office assistant in my small town.

Thanks to my jobs, I received two blessings: I obtained my driver's license and had the opportunity to travel extensively.

During these travels, I started capturing moments with my phone camera.

To be honest, I consider myself blessed in many ways. At my first job, I was fortunate to have an incredible team. They were my most extensive support system; we accomplished numerous milestones together. Through our triumphs and setbacks, we shared moments of joy and sorrow. You see, good colleagues are those who understand that "we" is more powerful than "me."

"Sometimes, you have to fall before you fly" Heather Long,
- Vicious Rebel

I adored the team I started with. Their mantra was simple: when we achieved success, we did it together, and when we faced challenges, we faced them together, too. This unity made us an exceptional team. Despite being younger, I was loved by my older colleagues, who showered me with love and support. One standout colleague, Hajni, became like a second mother to me. We could talk about anything, from work matters to personal issues.

Water droplets

What I loved most about the job was the unpredictability of each day. No two days were alike; this constant variety kept things exciting and far from boring. As a result, I improved rapidly, personally and professionally. After just a year, I was entrusted with overseeing the three northern regions a significant responsibility at 19. It meant a great deal to me that my managers valued my contributions. Additionally, I was honored to receive the Best Assistant award for my five years of service. The owners, who were French, were unfamiliar faces to me until that momentous day.

Boston - John Hancock Tower

Chapter 3

Exploring more-Finding Freedom Beyond Comfort

A long, calming road flanked by trees, with a car gliding along in peaceful solitude. It's the scene you've probably witnessed in countless movies, right? An artistic soul like mine yearns to wander and soak in the beauty of nature. That's why my journey led me from dancing to photography and eventually to traveling. I'm grateful to my job for giving me the opportunity to explore new places. They say, "Jobs fill your pocket, but adventures fill your soul." Thankfully, my jobs have filled both. Traveling transforms you into a storyteller, and I have many tales to share from my adventures on the road.

NYC night, my favorite picture was exhibited in Budapest

I traveled a lot in my country because of my new position. Our site office was in Baja, but we had some other site offices. Győr, Szombathely, Tatabánya, Kecskemét, Békéscsaba, Budapest. Our main office was in Szeged.

Above Budapest

When it comes to my favorite places, Tata holds a special spot in my heart. Its serene and tranquil atmosphere is truly captivating. One of my colleagues showed me Tata's hidden treasures.

Hungarian Parliament Building - Budapest

I adored my job and believed I would never want to leave. But as time passed, I longed for new challenges and greater responsibilities. The lack of fresh tasks and the monotony of the daily routine left me feeling uninspired. At a young age, I craved growth and excitement in my work.

Eventually, I decided to change jobs and became a zone manager at a cosmetics company. This new opportunity brought me much more than professional growth—it also introduced me to two incredible best friends. **Mónika and Otília.**

Széchenyi Chain Bridge - Budapest

And then, I made the move to Budapest. Honestly, I used to say I could never see myself living in Budapest. But in a surprisingly short time, I fell deeply in love with the city. I couldn't imagine my life anywhere else. I lived there for 3 years. My motto is "Life begins outside your comfort zone." I have always liked to push my limits. Finally, I found my dream job. I started as an administrative assistant at a solar panel company. I was nominated office manager after less than a year. I achieved everything that I wanted: self-confidence, success, financial independence. I was happy that I had achieved what I wanted.

Statue of Liberty

Then, I began to dream anew. No one can hinder your dreams. And my latest dream destination? New York City. Its image was plastered on my laptop screen, serving as my next goal.

Throughout my journey, my mom stood by me unwaveringly. While others cautioned, "Don't do it," she simply said, "Follow your heart and do what you want. I will always be here for you."

My dream spot in NYC old Pier 1

My mom visited me almost every month. We went to the cinema or the theater or just took a long walk around the city. One of my favorite tram lines was tram number 2. It runs along the Danube embankment between beautiful buildings. The light tram runs on this line every Christmas.

They are the memories I hold dear to my heart. From unconditional love to everyday wisdom, this list shows my mom's profound importance in my life.

My Lovely Mother

Chapter 4

Love in the City That Never Sleeps - A New Beginning

I truly believe in this, "Anything is possible when you have the right people there to support you." I've personally experienced it in my life, and when they say the greatest love stories often begin with falling in love with your best friend, I believe that, too. In fact, all great relationships start as friendships first. What do you think? My own love story is quite reminiscent of a movie plot. Our friendship began when I was 12 years old, and I was utterly fascinated by him, as only a 12-year-old can be. The nearly 8-year age difference between us seemed significant back then, but it's almost negligible nowadays.

My first self-portrait

As I mentioned earlier, I gravitated towards friendships with boys. Much to his mother's dismay, I hung out with them a lot. She worried about what the villagers would say if her adult son were seen with an underage girl. In our small community, where everyone knew everyone, there was one incident where his mother panicked and sent me home to play with my dolls. It was a very unpleasant experience then, but we just laugh about it now.

"It's better to be a lion for a day than a sheep all your life."
- Elizabeth Kenny

Music everywhere, forever, and always

I often ponder why girls are expected to play with dolls, even if they have no interest in them. It seems odd that every girl is supposed to have the same mindset and enjoy "girly" things.

Some enjoy many activities that girls usually wouldn't be interested in trying. I was one of them. Being a tomboy, you carry a tremendous attitude of "I don't care."

My favorite couple got married and I had the honor of photographing them

Good people come and go, and as we journey through the long road of life, we often find ourselves parting ways with old acquaintances while welcoming new ones. Such is the nature of life it keeps moving forward, with chapters ending and new ones beginning. We moved away from the village when I was 14, and our friendship was broken for a while. We occasionally spoke and met up, but I lost touch with him for almost ten years after that.

Oculus Center

He moved to New York, and I carried on living my own life. Each of us pursued our own dreams and built our own lives. Once again, I can't help but quote this: "Life isn't meant to be lived perfectly...but merely to be LIVED. Boldly, wildly, beautifully, uncertainly, imperfectly, magically LIVED." And that's exactly what I did during those years. Perhaps he was doing the same. We led separate lives with our own circles of acquaintances and unique circumstances until, one day; our paths crossed once again.

Fulton Street train station ceiling

People often speak about the curses of social media, but in my case, it proved to be a blessing. It was a fine day in 2019 when I rediscovered him on social media. So, indeed, social media has been a blessing for me. He noticed that I live in Budapest, which intrigued him, prompting him to initiate a conversation. He visited me in Budapest, and we spent a few days together. The former attraction between us quickly reignited. Our interest in each other was mutual, and we engaged in constant conversation. An inexplicable bond began to form between us, and it's astonishing how quickly we rediscovered each other. We laughed a lot, reflected on the good old days, and got to know each other again.

Old Pier 1. My favorite place in NYC

He lived in New York, my dream city, which was the cherry on top. He invited me, but not just for a vacation. We fell in love. I arrived in New York at the end of 2020 during the pandemic. My knowledge of English was close to zero. I feared this new world, but as I always say, life begins outside your comfort zone. So, why not? I left behind everything and followed my heart to New York. NYC is a lovely place for countless reasons, and when your loved one resides there, it becomes your own slice of heaven on earth. People adore NYC for its myriad attractions, and it's famous for saying, "New York City never sleeps." There's something about the air in New York that renders sleep irrelevant. Indeed, New York is not merely a city; it's an endlessly romantic notion. I could feel the love in the air, perhaps because my beloved was there. Regardless, despite all my fears and the significant change in my life, I felt happy to be there.

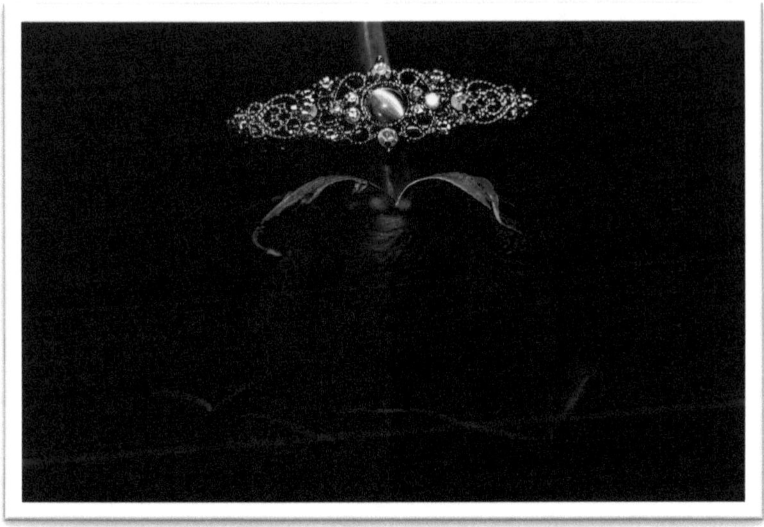

"One rose says more than a dozen." - Wendy Craig

"Every Flower is a soul blossoming in nature"

Chapter 5

Dreams Unlimited in NYC- Through the Lens of Love

New York is undeniably vibrant, and it's often said that Manhattan never sleeps. I thoroughly enjoyed my first few months in the city, filled with excitement as I explored its bustling streets and vibrant neighborhoods. While most cities are nouns, New York is a verb. I loved strolling its streets in silence, feeling like a character in a movie.

NYC after a huge storm from Pier 6

My partner gave me everything—home, love, and safety. For the first time in my life, I felt uncertain about what I wanted to do. Fortunately, he also had a keen eye for photography. Together, we began experimenting with a photography competition application. Through this, I found new friends and had the opportunity to practice and improve my English skills. Life is not always a bed of roses; there are good days and bad ones, too.

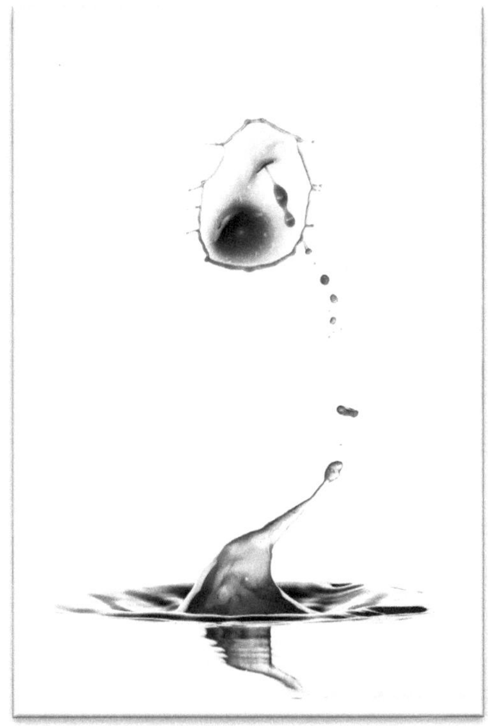

"A drop of water is as powerful as a thunder-bolt." - Thomas Huxley

As time went on I felt more and more uncomfortable not working. My savings were running low. And I felt the need to do something productive. However, my English skills were still relatively poor. I ended up working at a café, which turned out to be quite stressful. I often found myself alone during busy shifts, navigating awkward interactions with guests due to my limited language proficiency. Despite the challenges, this job was a valuable learning experience, helping me improve my English significantly. Eventually, I decided to move on and quit.

Great sunset in Florida

As I mentioned earlier, my partner provided me with everything I needed. He gifted me a professional camera, igniting a new passion within me. Determined to master photography, I learned everything about the camera and photography. I was scouring YouTube tutorials and learning from the experiences of other photographers. Three years ago, when I first held that professional camera in my hands, I felt a deep sense of fulfillment. I vividly recall my excitement during my initial TFP (Time for Print) portrait sessions.

Csabi is my first man model, I love his charm

Despite my limited proficiency in English at the time, I was eager to communicate my vision to my subjects and anxiously wondered if they would understand my instructions. "Will I understand what they say? Will they understand me, what I want from them?" This was a constant source of concern for me.

Timeless charm

I'm not currently doing my dream job, but I have a steady income from it. Meanwhile, I'm working on my photography aspirations. However, I'm hesitant to leave my current job and fully commit to building my photography career. Stepping out of my comfort zone in such a big way is daunting, and I fear failure. Of course, language also limits many things. I believe I need to deepen my knowledge of photography and gain more experience. Whenever I have the opportunity, I actively seek out new models to add to my portfolio. I'm constantly engaged in refining my skills and working on new projects.

"Beauty is a power; a smile is its sword" - John Ray

"A woman's greatest asset is her beauty." - Alex Comfort

My partner always encourages me. He says, "Quit your jobs, work full time on your dreams! You have nothing to worry about. We have a place to live, we have food to eat, we are healthy, we have everything!". Despite his support, something holds me back from taking that leap. He's a dedicated entrepreneur, running his own company, and I admire his work ethic. However, at times, I feel he pushes himself too hard. Whenever I can, I assist him with administrative tasks and find joy in contributing to his business.

When I say I learned everything about photography the hard way, I genuinely mean it. My Sony camera boasts a complex menu system, of which I've barely scratched the surface, maybe knowing only about 40% of its capabilities. Yet, despite this, I'm incredibly proud of the photos I produce. I can see the progression in my skills from where I started to where I am now. It's a journey that requires time, patience, and a lot of trial and error.

"Beauty awakens the soul act." - Dante Alighieri

Undoubtedly, Photography is a love affair with life. I love photographs because the best thing about them is that they never change, even when the people in them do. And if they do change, it's just as we wish through editing. How cool is that! Sometimes, I wish life could be edited as easily as a photograph. I suppose I've waxed philosophical enough for now. But this was all about my last trip outside my comfort zone: moving to New York. Now, I'm not sure if I'm ready for the next one just yet. I'm constantly striving to find a balance between my job and photography, but it's proving to be challenging.

Swarovski swan

Brand photoshoot

P.S. I love you

What I don't like is how time seems to operate differently here in New York. It's as if time flies by at an incredible pace. Days turn into weeks, weeks into months, and it feels like I'm just a passenger in my own life, not the captain. There are differences between us, like every individual, and naturally, these differences sometimes lead to friction in our relationship. I tend to be quite sensitive, but I consider myself lucky that my partner and I can discuss everything openly. While there are moments when we both lose our temper, we've always managed to come out through those situations successfully.

"Happiness is like a butterfly..." - Henry David Thoreau

I'm a coffee addict

I'd be lying if I said I never considered giving up and moving back to Hungary. But I'm not one to easily throw in the towel. I've come to realize that I'm not quite the same person I used to be. A person is lost, the person with a wandering soul, an artistic and creative mind, and a heart full of unlimited dreams and adventures always on the mind. I don't blame my partner or New York City for this transformation, but living in a relationship inevitably changes you, even if your partner doesn't ask you to. That's just part of the package of being in a relationship.

"Cats are connoisseurs of comfort." - James Herriot

Cityscape above you

I feel a little lost now, and I'm in the process of rediscovering myself. I want to reconnect with my old self, the one filled with dreams and aspirations. It's a work in progress, but I'm determined to get there eventually. Though sometimes I may lose sight of the goal and veer off track, I always find my way back.

Abounded prison in Philadelphia

"A flower blossom for its own joy"

Chapter 6

A Photographic Journey of Self-Discovery - Ups
and Downs

Do you have something or someone that serves as your driving force in life, propelling you forward?

It's that one thing that pulls us back when we feel lost and keeps us moving forward. For me, it's photography. There have been times when I lost a bit of interest, especially during periods of depression when even our favorite things can lose their appeal. But overcoming those challenges helps us realign with our passions, clarifying our likes and dislikes and guiding us back on track.

Albany City Hall

Passion is only possible with practice and mastery. I realized I needed to delve deeper into photography, expanding my knowledge and skills. Building my portfolio was a priority, but finding good models was hard, especially since I was not yet an established photographer. Once again, social media came to my rescue, and I saw an ad by Norbert Bánhalmi there. I learned a lot about portraits and street photography from him.

The iron teeth of time

Boston cityscape

Al Capone's prison

I found out that he was looking for models during his trip to New York. I thought there should be a new series about myself and how much easier it is to learn if I am the model. I wrote to him that I would be his model if he had a free spot. We started talking about photography, and I told him I had started my photography journey, too. Even without seeing my portfolio, he said he would happily work with me for a few days during his trip to New York, offering practical tips. I was thrilled. I'm lucky that I often encounter good people. Thank you, Lord, for your blessings on my life.

Chicago cityscape

I invited him to our home and, in return, received a 5-day intensive course from him. We went together, and I got the opportunity to accompany him on most of his photo shoots. I learned about camera settings and poses, listened to his conversations with the models, and observed the questions he asked. He opened my eyes to the exciting aspects of street photography.

"When you see a good move, look for a better one."
- Emanuel Lasker

Additionally, I had the opportunity to accompany him to a boudoir photo shoot. It was a very different experience for me. A boudoir session is a luxurious photo experience conducted in a bedroom setting to lift feelings of romance and richness. It's more than just a lingerie photoshoot; it's a reminder that you are courageous and strong. This experience taught me a lot.

But, I actually realized that it's not my world, perhaps because I'm not content with my own body. This will be another trip out of my comfort zone again to make friends with how I look.

"The Earth laughs in flowers." - Ralph Waldo Emerson

After an intensive five days of study, I knew I wanted to pursue this, but I understood it would be a long journey. Norbert Bánhalmi helped me start my website, and now I have a beautiful platform that I constantly refine. Through this journey, I've made many photographer friends who have helped me continue to improve. We've taken numerous photos together, and they've shared tricks and taught me about studio lighting settings and many other valuable techniques. From still-life photography to water collision photography to low-key portrait lighting. Thanks to them for their unwavering support.

The dog is the people's best friend

Nowadays, I pursue photography as a hobby, occasionally receiving requests for portrait shoots. Recently, an Indonesian fashion brand, CapBali, approached me to do a photoshoot. It was a great pleasure to see my New York photographs showcased along the catwalk and in the shop window during the presentation of their new collection.

Minimalist street photography with my Love

One of my favorite portrait styles is the Low-Key portrait. Stunning pictures are created with a black background, one or two flashlights, and a well-posed model. I love the dramatic lighting of this style, as it effortlessly conveys any emotion. When I was younger, I really liked the black outfits. Both my mom and my second mom from my job often reminded me that black isn't a color, and they always asked me to change my clothes. I loved the moody black clothes, and it seems that this preference is reflected in my photo shoot as well.

Our first TFP session with Val

Stunning studio flower

I particularly enjoy the predominantly black compositions. Although humans perceive reality in colors, for me, black and white photography has always been linked to an image's more profound truth and hidden essence. And you see, human nature is not simply black and white; it's a spectrum of black and grey. Black holds a special place as my favorite color, symbolizing depth and mystery.

However, Life is not just black and white; it's also infused with shades of gray, adding nuance and complexity to our experiences.

Low-key family portrait

Given my affinity for black, I naturally gravitate towards low-key portrait photography. These photos utilize low-key lighting techniques, producing images characterized by dim lighting and predominantly dark tones. Light is strategically directed onto specific subject areas, crafting a mysterious and dramatic ambiance within the portrait. Everything seems simpler in black and white, with fewer distractions and more attractions.

Mostly black flower

Just like my photos, I am a low-key person. I like my privacy. "Not everyone needs to know everything about me, so I choose to stay low-key." I like this quote by Hendri Fahrezi because my English was very poor when I came to New York, and I wanted to stay low-key. I wanted to be invisible. Usually, I like talking, but it was a tough part in New York. I couldn't practice one of my favorite passions. My partner and I enjoy dancing bachata, but I vividly recall our first dinner with the team. I found myself mostly listening, unable to interject into the conversation because they had long since gone elsewhere by the time I figured out what I wanted to say. It was awkward, and I could sense the question marks on many people's faces. They didn't understand why I kept my distance. They know what happened back then, and I'm glad I can talk with them now. Even though there are still days when I prefer to keep a low profile, I enjoy engaging in passionate conversations when we're with friends. However, I always reserve a part of myself for the low-key love.

Chicago night - Wrigley Building

Chapter 7

A World of Art and Photography - Beauty, Gratitude and Adventure

As I told you earlier, I've been lucky enough to meet many amazing people who opened my eyes to the world of art and photography. Photography is a whole different world—a world of beauty and ugliness, perfection and imperfection, the real and the surreal. Once you immerse yourself in this world and delve deeper, your entire perception and vision transform profoundly, turning 180 degrees. I look at the people, objects, and buildings around me differently today.

Sunbathing

I'm constantly on the lookout for new, unique, and stunning faces to add to my portfolio. Whenever my camera is with me, I approach strangers and ask them to be my models. I introduce myself as a photographer and express what I admire about them. I show them my portfolio and request their permission to photograph them. Afterwards, I send them the pictures.

Long exposure street photography with my Love

My goal is always to capture the beauty that I see in people. Kim Namjoon once said, "No one is born ugly; we're just born in a judgmental society." It's exactly how I feel. I truly believe that, in physical terms, there is not a single person in the world who is ugly. Each individual possesses their own unique beauty, even if it may not be immediately apparent to everyone. Beauty is subjective, and everyone is attractive to someone. I have never looked at someone and thought, "Damn, they're ugly." For me, true ugliness lies within a person's character—cruelty, intolerance, and general negativity make someone truly unattractive. We are all like unique pieces of art, each with our own story to tell. Every line, scar, stretch mark, and imperfection contributes to our beauty and makes us who we are.

My first dog portrait

A photographer, an artist, or a creative soul may have a different perspective. Sometimes, I have time to be a tourist in my city, so I just pick up my camera and go to my favorite places or explore something unknown. Despite living here for three years, I still have yet to discover many places. Sometimes, I actively seek out subjects to photograph, while other times, interesting scenes naturally present as I go about my day. I find myself drawn to capturing intriguing shadows, sunlight, and reflections. Although I enjoy photographing architecture, I need to delve deeper into this genre.

Pemaquid Point Lighthouse in Maine

I think a photographer can see what is invisible to others. The world is like an inexhaustible art to me. From the myriad colors of flowers to the visible history embedded in buildings, from the hidden treasures of nature to the stunning vistas of cities, from the diverse animal kingdom to the intricate details of the macro world, even the everyday objects in a kitchen or a simple cup of coffee—all of these hold beauty waiting to be captured through the lens of a camera. Achieving good results in a world filled with professional photographers has fueled my desire to pursue this dream further. It's what I want to dedicate myself to wholeheartedly. I aim to capture every significant moment for people, preserving them for eternity. Through photography, I've realized that I possess a superpower—I can freeze time. I've learned there is beauty in everything, waiting to be captured, even in its perfect imperfection. I believe that no two photographers are alike; each is limited only by their imagination. Photography is an art; the key is finding your own style which brings you joy.

"Smile is the beauty of the soul." - Lailah Gifty Akita

There are several memories that I love to share, and they always please me. One of my favorite moments was when my mom visited me in New York for the first time. She was here for a month. Despite not liking pictures of herself, I asked her to be my model. I'll never forget the smile on her face; she laughed a lot as we took photos. We were at the Top of the Rock Rockefeller Center, witnessing an incredible sunset together. I want to cherish this moment forever.

My artistic mind captured that moment, and my smart camera preserved it in their memories.

One of my favorite memories with my Mom in NYC

This is all we can wish for: joyous moments, fond memories, the presence of loved ones, the beauty of nature, and the blessing of health, both mental and physical. Gratitude fills my heart for all these blessings. A million thanks, indeed. I would quote Gretchen Rubin that,

"One of the best ways to make yourself happy in the present is to recall happy times from the past. Photos are a great memory prompt, and because we tend to take photos of happy occasions, they weigh our memories to the good."

When I recall my good memories, my trips and adventures are always unforgettable. As they say, "Adventure is important in life. Making memories matters. Effort from imagination and following adventure creates stories that you keep forever. And anyone can do it."(Rob Lowe). One trip to Maine stands out prominently. It significantly enriched my portfolio. Before our visit, my portfolio lacked images of lighthouses. I gifted this trip to my love for his birthday, and we affectionately dubbed ourselves "Lighthouse hunters."

Annisquam Harbor Light Station in Maine

We spent six days in Maine in 3 different cities. We captured images of 12 lighthouses, making it an incredible journey together. While we discovered some breathtaking places and views, the trip also presented its fair share of challenges.

Minneapolis train station

Nonetheless, I cherished every moment of it. Our souls were filled with new experiences while our bodies, dead tired, returned home from the trip. Now I understand why people say you need to take an extra week off after a trip.

One of my favorite portrait sessions was with Val. We first met when I was building my portfolio, and I instantly adored her. She's not only beautiful but also creative and talented as a model. Her movements are natural and graceful in front of the camera, almost like she's softly floating.

If you must wear a mask, wear something sparkly

Sometimes, I find myself unable to stop capturing photos when we're working together. One of our standout styles was the African studio shoot. She was the perfect model I had ever met. One day, after seeing something similar on social media, I was inspired to create our own version, and the result was simply stunning. Everything came together perfectly, from the clothes and makeup to the mood and her expressions. I simply love it. I always look forward to working with her.

Yin and Yang harmony

African style with my awesome model

There is a long series of memories in its journey, and I will definitely create more in the future. As a photographer and a memory maker, my eyes are open to everything. I press the button if I see something I want to preserve forever. "We didn't realize we were making memories. We just knew we were having fun." (A.A. Milne).

Chapter 8

The Wow Factor - Elevating Photography Beyond Expectations

If you have even a passing interest in photography, you may have heard of György Stalter and his wife, M Horváth Judit. They are renowned Hungarian photographers, celebrated for their multiple award-winning work. György Stalter is known for his masterpieces Aranyélet (2015), Kills On Wheels (2016), and Things Worth Weeping For (2021). Their work is truly remarkable and exceptional in every aspect.

Feel the music

"A real ballerina must fill her space with her own personality."
- Natalia Makarova

Once, I had the opportunity to speak with them. I was working for their daughter then, and they happened to visit her. I was lucky to be in the right place at the right time. They generously shared valuable pieces of advice with me, such as how to crop my pictures effectively and what to consider when editing them. I even had the opportunity to take a photo of their grandson, and they were amazed at how I managed to highlight his eyes in the picture. When they looked at my photos, they just said, "You are doing this much more seriously than we thought." Their words were exactly what I needed to hear at that moment. From then on, I aspired to elicit the same "wow" factor from others with my work.

Underwater world

Nowadays, everyone fancies themselves a photographer. Smartphone cameras have certainly had an impact on the photography industry. The accessibility and convenience of smartphones empowered people to capture and share stunning images effortlessly, bypassing the need for specialized equipment or technical know-how. This surge in amateur photography has intensified competition, particularly in fields like event and portrait photography.

The eye is the mirror of the soul

However, professional photographers remain indispensable in specific domains such as commercial, fashion, and fine art photography, where technical expertise and creative vision are paramount. A former studio photographer, Charles Haacker, explains this by saying,

"I do not know for sure, but logic suggests that professionals must be losing work to cell phones and point-and-shoots because of their ubiquity, especially in Western culture. In the US, 90% of the population has a cell phone with a camera. When I was working, long before digital, pros lost some business to eager amateurs with sophisticated cameras (whether they really knew how to use them or not) but the P&S of that day could not produce anything like what even a "prosumer" camera of the era could.

Everyone who lived in the "old days" wondered anxiously if their Instamatic pictures would "come out." You had no clue until the film was processed and printed. Often, you would see frames that were completely blank. Today, with a cell phone, you practically have to work at it to mess up a picture. You see on your screen what the picture will look like. If your finger has drifted in front of the lens

Lovely dog

I agree that today's smartphones have great cameras, and if
someone has a good eye, they can create fantastic things even
without a professional camera. Recently, if I tell someone that "I'm

a photographer," they will wave one, but when I show my work, the wow factor comes. Of course, I want to impress people with my work because it feels good when someone recognizes that what I do is beautiful.

Calm under the pier

I'm repeating myself now: I think no two photographers are alike. Everyone is bound by their own imagination and perspective. Photography is an art. You just have to find your style what makes you happy. A perfect example of this is my partner and me. There have been numerous instances where we perceive things differently. I have a particular photo of the Brooklyn Bridge that he has never entirely understood why I captured it. However, I love this image, and it has received positive feedback, affirming the diversity of artistic interpretation. There are indeed guidelines to follow in photography, but there are no hard and fast rules about when or how to apply them.

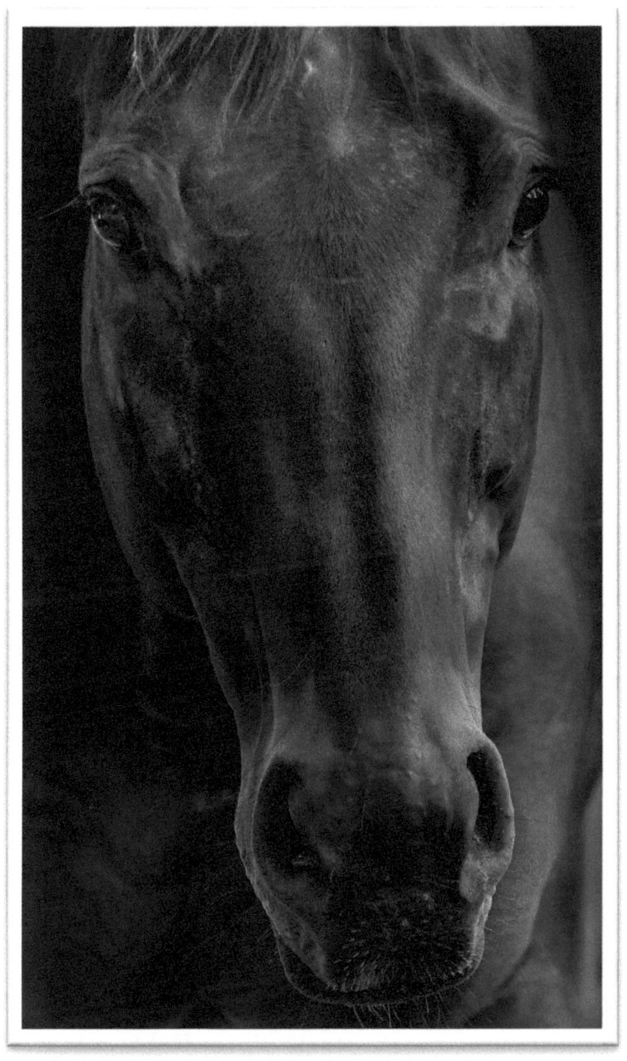

"Horses lend us the wings we lack." - Pam Brown

I take pictures of everything that I like. Since I've mastered Photoshop better, our editing process and style are different too. When working on commissioned projects, I always consider the client's preferences. However, I stick to my personal style for TFP (Time for Print) or spontaneous photo shoots. I really like incorporating the matte effect into my photos, although I'm aware that many people don't like it. Personally, I'm drawn to cooler tones, but I understand that many prefer warmer hues. Ultimately, the direction I take often depends on my mood and how I see the image in front of me.

A courageous, intelligent dog

This is exactly how we see the bigger picture of life. Troubles and difficulties inevitably arise, but it's our response that defines our experience. We can either choose to remain cool or allow ourselves to become overwhelmed by the challenges we face. So why not stay calm and figure out ways to overcome them? It's been my guiding mantra throughout life.

Coney Island firework

When I started photography, one of the most difficult things for me was learning editing programs. When I first saw Photoshop, I said I would never learn this. I started with Lightroom, slowly learning it step by step. However, as time passed, I found myself unable to imagine life without Photoshop. I particularly appreciate its black-and-white infinity tools, which allow me to effortlessly generate hundreds of variations from a single image with just one click. Black and white photography holds a special place in my heart because it's more emotional than the color pictures. There are moments when I perceive the world through a monochromatic lens, especially during times of sadness. But I know that behind every cloud, the sun continues to shine. There is always a ray of hope, no matter how dark it may seem.

As I mentioned earlier, I often envision the composition in black and white when I take pictures. I also talked about my favorite portrait style, the low-key portrait. The dramatic lighting adds depth to the image. Today, I would describe myself as a hobby photographer, but I enjoy every moment I spend behind the lens. I'm steadily making progress on my journey.

"You can seduce a man without taking anything off, without even touching him." - Rae Dawn Chong

Orangutan is a wise old man of the jungle

Chapter 9

The Art of Editing - A Thing of Beauty is a Joy Forever

I work with a Sony camera, and I particularly appreciate the vibrant colors it produces. However, I've come to realize that the type of camera you use doesn't define your skill as a photographer. What truly matters is your imagination and your ability to find beauty in everything you photograph. A common saying is "Beauty is in the eye of the beholder," which suggests that beauty is subjective and is perceived differently by each individual observer.

"The earth laughs in flowers." - Ralph Waldo Emerson

You can start to capture the beauty with a cheaper starter camera. Once you understand how it works and what you need for stunning photos, you can decide which camera is best for you. Just go outside and look forward to capturing memories of your trips, family, small things, huge things—anything that catches your eye. I, myself, feel great joy in it.

How beautifully John Keats expressed this in his famous poem:

A thing of beauty is a joy for ever:

Its loveliness increases; it will never

Pass into nothingness; but still will keep

A bower quiet for us, and a sleep

Full of sweet dreams, and health, and quiet breathing.

Therefore, on every morrow, are we wreathing

A flowery band to bind us to the earth,

Spite of despondence, of the inhuman dearth

Of noble natures, of the gloomy days,

Of all the unhealthy and o'er-darkened ways

"In joy or sadness, flowers are our constant friends."

Then comes the art of editing. You often don't get the image you want to see back on the camera, but post-processing will achieve what you saw on the spot. You don't have to invest in the most expensive editing programs immediately; there are plenty of free options available. The key is to dedicate time to editing your images.

Sometimes, I feel like I haven't decided yet what kind of photographer I want to be. Right now, I'm exploring everything, everywhere. I'm always trying out new equipment, too. Every time I try a new lens, I'm filled with excitement. Every lens is different, and you must learn how to use them effectively. I remember when I first tried the macro lens. I said I would never use manual focus, but now I can't live without it. I love capturing images of flowers, insects, and water droplets; for me, there's no better option than manual focus. Through photography, I've also learned that you can master anything if you're genuinely interested. As they say, "A journey of a thousand miles begins with a single step." So, it's all about taking the first step in the right direction. Don't give up; follow your heart and dreams. There are better days and not-so-good days, but it's always worth it. Every experience is valuable; you can learn a lot, even from the bad ones, because all genuine learning comes through experience. Sometimes, I consider myself too rational; I like to see my goal, but often, I want to take two steps instead of one. My partner always says, "It is enough if you see the next step towards where you want to go."

"Be a flamingo in a flock of pigeons." - Savannah Larsen

All big dreams throughout history have come true through wild and illogical thinking. Even Albert Einstein said, "I never made one of my discoveries through the process of rational thinking."

I often find myself impatient, and that's probably one of the most frustrating aspects of my personality. If you want to avoid disappointment as many times as I have, it's important to give yourself time. I'm working hard to be more patient myself.

Chicago night lights

Zénó is the best dog model

Chapter 10

Sky's the limit - Following all your dreams

I wandered lonely as a cloud
That floats on high o'er vales and hills,
When all at once I saw a crowd,
A host of golden daffodils;
Beside the lake, beneath the trees,
Fluttering and dancing in the breeze.

Continuous as the stars that shine
And twinkle on the Milky Way,
They stretched in never-ending line
Along the margin of a bay:
Ten thousand saw I at a glance,
Tossing their heads in sprightly dance.

The other night, I found a girl wandering, much like a cloud as in William Wordsworth's poem. Though that shy, hesitant little girl has grown into a confident professional, she still carries the soul of a wanderer deep inside her. Looking back today, I feel grateful that the career I started at 18 has taken me so far, with many achievements along the way. I always had everything I really needed. I worked extensively on my personality through breathing therapy and Bach flower therapy. I used to be quick to anger and often spoke without thinking, causing lasting harm to those I love. I desired change because I wanted to create space for love, and one fine day, life brought love into my life. What I wasn't prepared for was that someone 4,000 miles away would capture my heart, but it happened. We discussed a lot about how different life is in America, and without proficient language skills, the opportunities were much fewer than in Hungary.

The tulip is nature's apology for winter

I thought I had finally met someone I had desired all my life; everything seemed aligned, so why not take a giant leap to see how our life together would unfold? However, I learned that the reality of living and experiencing something entirely different was quite challenging. It wasn't hard to let go of my previous life, but coming to terms with the fact that I had to rebuild myself and my career from a much lower starting point in New York was daunting. I've lived here for three years. There are still days when my ego whispers, "Hey, this isn't you." I'm working on finding my path and rebuilding a career that I can once again be proud of. Fortunately, my partner is already so proud of me and what I've achieved in these three years.

He always reminds me that even small successes should be celebrated.

Boston - John Hancock Tower

If you want to achieve your dreams, you have to work hard for them. Good and bad days come and go in cycles. I often have to remind myself that tough times eventually pass. Unfortunately, by nature, I tend to be impatient. I often overwhelm myself by pursuing too many things simultaneously, only to realize later that I still need to complete something. Achieving your dreams requires dedicating quality time and effort. My mom often encourages me to dream big. There should be no limits to your dreams, but you also have to take action to make them a reality.

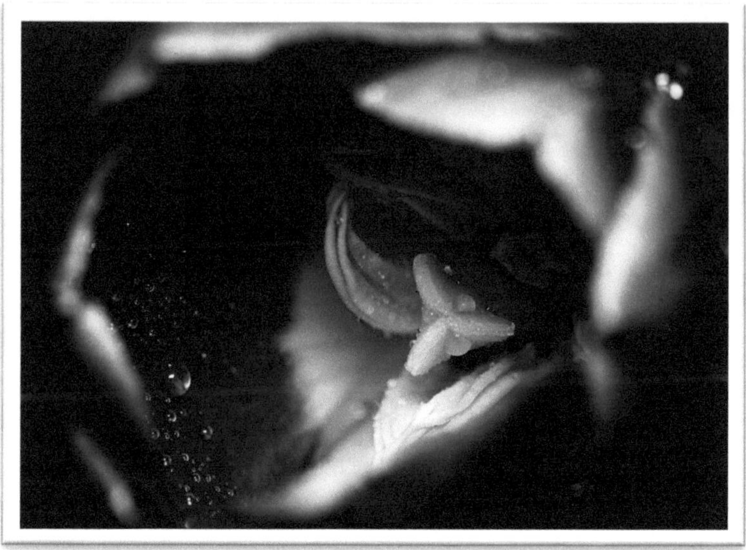

"Where flowers bloom so does hope." - Lady Bird Johnson

Now, I want to explore the world, travel more, and witness unique places. Although I've had many of my photographs exhibited in almost all parts of the world, I now aspire to have my own exhibition featuring the pictures published in this book so I can feel an even closer connection to them. I'm on the lookout for a suitable venue. Meanwhile, I continue to expand my portfolio, hoping that my path as a photographer will become more apparent to me one day. In the meantime, I seek beauty in everything and cherish each moment, making memories along the way. I find contentment in celebrating small successes and am setting new milestones to strive for.

Cathedral of Saint Paul

My message to my readers is that the desire to improve and push one's limits raises a person to a level they can't even imagine in their dreams. So, everyone should push the boundaries of their comfort zone and always learn something new. Always follow your dreams. I try to live my life accordingly, and I love my dreams.

I began my story with a dream, one of the many dreams that my wandering soul frequently sees- dreams of a shining, rising, and flourishing girl in a beautiful meadow, dreams of a little dancing girl in the small town of Bátaszék, dreams of the beautiful Siófok, where a tomboyish girl cycles along shores of Lake Balaton, dreams of a teenager dancing on the stage of a community center in Vaskút, dreams where a hesitant girl roamed the streets of bustling NYC.

Then, there are some surreal dreams of a black-and-white world where a girl hesitates to face people and hides behind a big black rock.

Dreams of hiking, capturing, loving, and envying. Yes, my dear folks! My wandering soul is always on trips in dreams. They are numerous and limitless. They are dreams unlimited through the lens of life that I tried to share with you in this autobiography!

Beauty in the minimalist

"The soul is like a violin string: it makes music only when it is stretched." - Neal A. Maxwell

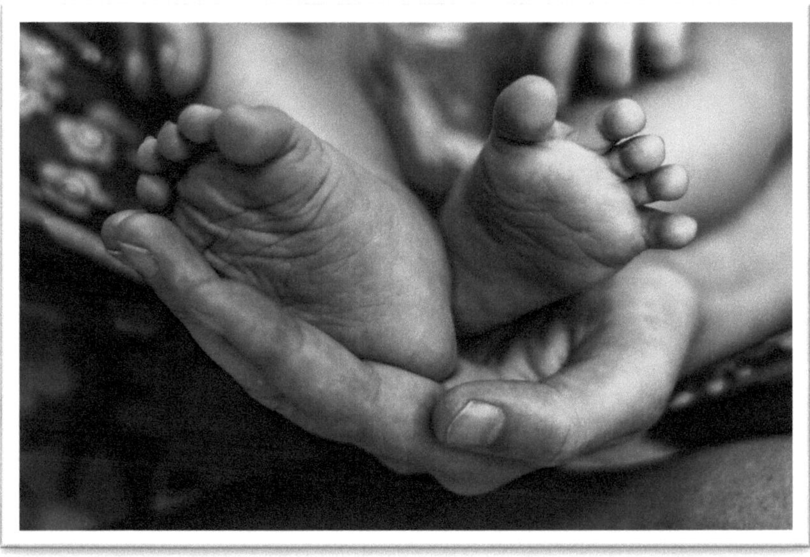

"A mother's arms are more comforting than anyone else's." - Princess Diana

International exhibitions:

Very Best of Black & White

Exhibition dates: 23 Sep - 4 Nov 2022 Bridgeport Art Center, Chicago, USA

https://gurushots.com/challenge/very-best-of-black-white1/winners/all

Black & White Photographer of the Year

Exhibition dates: 1-3 June, 2023 Coningsby Gallery London, UK

https://gurushots.com/challenge/black-white-photographer-of-the-year1/winners/all

Art of Black & White

Exhibition Dates: 9-11 June, 2023 Johannesburg, South Africa

https://gurushots.com/challenge/art-of-black-white8/winners/all

Very Best of Black & White

Exhibition dates: 19-22 October, 2023 Art Market Budapest Hungary

https://gurushots.com/challenge/very-best-of-black-white3/winners/all

Art of Black & White

Exhibition Dates: 22-24 September 2023 6x6 Centre for Photography in Limassol, Cyprus

https://gurushots.com/challenge/art-of-black-white10/winners/all

Art of Black & White

Exhibition Dates: 3-6 February, 2024 Modeka Gallery in beautiful Manila, Philippines

https://gurushots.com/challenge/art-of-black-white12/winners/all

Magazine publications:

Mostly Black Creative Light Issue 47.

Page 71.

https://issuu.com/julieoswin/docs/issue-47?fr=sNGQ1YzQ2NDM5NDM

Mostly Black Practical Photoshop magazine Issue 135. June 2022.

Page 39.

Mostly Black Practical Photoshop magazine Issue 142. January 2023.

Page 31.

https://gurushots.com/challenge/mostly-black7/winners/all

Mostly Black Photography Week Magazine Issue 557. 25-31 May 2023.

Page 17.

https://gurushots.com/challenge/mostly-black11/winners/all

The Portrait Art Square Gallery September 2. 2023.

https://artspaces.kunstmatrix.com/en/exhibition/10879171/the-portrait

The Still Life Art Square Gallery September 16. 2023.

https://artspaces.kunstmatrix.com/en/exhibition/12202162/the-still-life

Online Articles:

https://www.digitalcameraworld.com/features/gurushots-winning-photos-from-the-mostly-black-competition

Street Photography

https://121clicks.com/inspirations/gurushots-street-photography-photo-challenge

https://gurushots.com/challenge/street-photography26/winners/all

Mostly Black

https://www.digitalcameraworld.com/features/winning-photos-from-the-gurushots-mostly-black-competition

Nature photography

https://121clicks.com/interviews/hungarian-nature-photographer-viktoria-farkas

Monochrome Photography Award

International Black & White Photography Contest

FINE ART: HONORABLE MENTION 2023

https://monoawards.com/winners-gallery/monochrome-awards-2023/amateur/fine-art/hm/19611

Many thanks to my Love, who is always by my side and helps me in everything; to my lovely Mom, who always believes in me unconditionally; to my Hungarian friends Ildi, Móni, Otília who, even if we don't talk every day, are always there for me, and last but not least, thanks to my friend MiZsu, who here in America helps me not to go crazy and to find my way.